"'The darkness' is coming for us—the darkness of sin, of loss and of forgetfulness, of who we are and who God is. And yet, just when you want to shut the darkness out, James Matthew Wilson invites us to crack open our hearts 'so truth may not die in the ear / But, suitably disguised, appear.' Just when you think you know something—a lilac, a garden, the Church, a tow-truck driver— Wilson entices us to look closer. Within every created thing, person, or place dwells a mystery to behold, a surprise for us if we can stay attentive and humble. In *Saint Thomas and the Forbidden Birds*, Wilson offers us a holy resistance to the darkness coming—to swap our narrow and limited vision for eyes infused with grace."

—**Colleen Hutt**, Director of Vision and Outreach,
Well-Read Mom

"James Matthew Wilson is a treasure. Without making demands, his sublime poetry beckons us softly to remember who we are: children of God in a miraculous world. In a harried age of forever 'becoming,' Wilson's words invite us to rest awhile in the healing moments of simply 'being.' That is quite a balm for a reeling, uncertain world."

—**Tod Worner**, Managing Editor of *Evangelization & Culture*

Saint Thomas
AND THE
Forbidden Birds

Saint Thomas
AND THE
Forbidden Birds

JAMES MATTHEW WILSON

Published by Word on Fire, Elk Grove Village, IL 60007
© 2024 by James Matthew Wilson
Printed in the United States of America
All rights reserved

Cover design by Cassie Bielak, typesetting by Marlene Burrell,
and interior art direction by Nicolas Fredrickson

First printing, April 2024

ISBN: 978-1-68578-094-4

Library of Congress Control Number: 2023946604

For Hilary
Once Again

Form is the ultimate gift that love can offer—
The vital union of necessity
With all that we desire, all that we suffer.

—Adrienne Rich

The Son of man, when he cometh, shall he find, think you,
faith on earth?

—Luke 18:8 (Douay-Rheims)

Contents

To an Unborn Child

Storm clouds move in and darken all the house,
　　The morning paper on the kitchen table dim,
Where I've been reading some reporter's grouse
　　At things already bad, now growing grim.
　　Most of the prodigies agree with him.

I rise to light a lamp, and hear the thunder,
　　And watch the first drops thudding on the lawn.
Your mother joins me. Here we stand, in wonder,
　　Between the hour that marks your life's first dawn
　　And that one, still obscure, we're counting on.

1

We are not in the same place after all.
The only evidence of the disaster,
Mapping out across the bedroom wall.
     —A.E. Stallings

When the second raid came at sunset, I was holding
a glass of burgundy with strawberries floating in it.
The city, with its red towers and domes, was a place
of stupendous beauty, like a calyx that they fly over to
accomplish their deadly act of pollination.
     —Ernst Jünger

Self-Possession

This girl in heels walks by a mirror
   And stops to sweep hair from her shoulder,
Then turns and goes, as if it's clear her
   Fate is to be her own beholder,
And that glass in the hall grows clearer
   With her approach, and dimmed and older
Deprived and emptied of the face
Whose visitation was its grace.

With a firm setting of his jaw,
   And straightened back, the youth may steel
Himself against the threat of awe
   To loose his flabby soul and peel
Away composure, lest some raw
   Sensation rob him of what's real.
Thus armed and solid, he'd appear
To her whose beauty wanders near.

Others may call it all deceit:
   The buoyant body, air of grace,
The mannered greeting, slow retreat
   Of hands, the raised repose of face;
Those frail and viscous hearts that greet
   The world lie hidden in a case,
Losing what life they seek to gain
Immured from all such honest pain.

But, heart, who wait in cloistral dark,
    And strive to beat in measured tune,
You lend the decent form its spark
    While it sustains you when you swoon,
Gives to thought's flight its well-aimed arc,
    And writes what from sense fades too soon,
So truth may not die in the ear
But, suitably disguised, appear.

The Garden

The grass beneath my step is dry and sifts
To ash as I trudge back to check the garden
For new growth. Far above, the sky's blank blue
Retreats before the fiery eye that rules it.
I know what all this is a symbol of;
My brother's lands are burning in the West.
     But in the ordered bed of cedar ties
I built, then planted with an amateur's
Stupidity a dozen kinds of seeds,
All is grown wild and winding in profusion.
Tomato leaves overwhelm their rounded trellis
And trace on hand and lip a rich tobacco.
Cucumber vines, hollow and bristly, wind
Among the spreading pumpkins, back and forth,
Them both a mess of orange flower and fat leaf.
Their curling tendrils latch on any stem
In reach, and draw the anaheims and bells
Beneath a canopy to starve in shade.
They'd throttle everything, till, when they've grown
Too far from their first root, the ants will come
And nimbly trot the stiff and moldering veins
To suck the pestilential milk of aphids.
     I clip them back, uncovering carrot fronds
Sprayed from their bald tops crowning in the soil.
I see dark melons spill their seedy guts.
     Oh, yes, we lower our eyes from brilliant things,
When they stand glowering in their airy strangeness,
And think that little order we have made

Will shelter us—will do for all we need.
But what's sown from our hand grows well beyond
Such well-trimmed plotting and, in this, it tells
That every order—though the roots be slow,
And though leaves curl and wither in the noon—
Is rooted in a broader spread profusion
Than any easy measure we may make;
And which we don't defy or much improve
But stand, uncomprehending parts, within.

M.A.C.

East Lansing, Michigan

On either side, the highway's barren stretch
Is dwarfed by sweeping wastes of prairie grass,
Its pale dry leaves beneath dark heads of vetch
And clumps of sumac shimmering like glass.

To look on this, you'd think man had just come,
Bloomed with the Queen Anne's lace, and will not last;
What little he set down as soon succumb
To stands of pine and maple or wind's blast.

But, if you see the little streets erupt
On ancient marsh, the pool hall and brick church,
Where we boys grew both conscious and corrupt
Dispelling boredom, entering on the search

For just what sort of men we should become,
You'll learn the place is thick with ghosts, is haunted
By faces kissed, fists thrown, and words that drum
Through time, as we sought what it was we wanted.

Return to Saint Thomas

Here we are, with five children we've amassed,
   The nave a bloated hull of tin, the cross
   Dangling from double chains, its weight of loss
Moored in midair as listing decades passed.
A few gray heads, behind, recall a past
   When that bright-sharded window cast a gloss
   On pews packed full: however time's waves toss
The Church, it bears its people to the last.

That's not the obvious lesson it once seemed,
   As I turn toward strange faces offering peace,
   And fail to find those who were borne with me
Through all the sacraments, those taught to see,
   In every fall, a chance to be redeemed,
   Never suspecting prayer might simply cease.

Lilacs

You stand beneath the lilac bush at night
   And smell her heavy blossoms, think, *ah, right,*
I've caught this scent a thousand times before,
   Which, subtle though it is, you can't ignore.
It fills the mind and yet escapes it too,
   As every mystery worth the name will do.
Perhaps that's why, like baby faces, ants,
   The curious innards of a marshland's plants;
Like love songs or the neighbor's lab you pet,
   No matter how familiar, we still get
A pulse of wonder and a hint of fear
   That some ethereal visitant draws near.

Twilight

Raw and naïve, I was once told,
    As a friend quietly marked her birthday,
She felt relief at growing old.

In youth, the weight of what's unknown
    Overloads the pan and wrecks the scale,
Till life seems anxiousness alone.

No matter how much we may savor,
    Writes Hobbes, still more lies round to fear:
War, want, or losing some god's favor.

Around her ever briefer rest,
    The early autumn twilight fell
And time stood by in darkness dressed.

Cracks

1

The heads of maples filling in above,
She sets out on her daylight wanderings,
Some tarnished pennies stored in one old glove
She grips to feel its weight as her arm swings.

A jealous grip perhaps—and yet she's skipping
And humming notes that spread beyond all tune,
Her dress like floating clouds through green fields
    slipping,
And eyes as brightened as a summer moon.

Along her way, she stops, from time to time,
To draw a penny from its woolen sack;
As if to plant the earth with what's sublime
She'll press it down within a sidewalk crack.

11

The guests expected and the kitchen warm
With ham and bubbling green bean casserole,
The woman turned and, taking up his arm,
Reminded him the table would be full.

She pressed the near end firmly to her side,
While he took hold and pulled upon the far,
To spread the surface outward on its slide
And make room for the leaf with inlaid star.

But as the cherry top was drawn apart,
They saw the grime of ancient apple sauce
And other seeping things, whose cunning art
Had hid their moldering as a grove does moss.

III

All fissures that run through our sunlit visions;
All chips in polished marble, nicks in paint;
All hints our logic covers up elisions
And every perfect surface is a feint;

All places out of reach beneath the stove,
Where ballpoint pens or uncooked rice have rolled;
Each pause in speech that opens like a cove
Between the easily said and the untold;

All darkness that's as painful as the light
To see and not see with the pulsing eye;
We feel your presences beyond our sight
And hear your breath beneath the May wind's cry.

Ambition

Halfway along in reading a new life
Of Dante, I'm still marveling at the man's
Conviction he's been set apart for greatness,
    Though of its form

He's still unsure. So far, in fact, he's marred
Most that he's tried and left the rest unfinished,
Promising nonetheless some lasting work
    Not yet begun.

I bend still closer to the page, my mind
Halting before a pride it can't quite fathom.
So it was with the climbing Dante, stopped,
    Hunched down, to speak

With the famed illustrator he found crawling
Beneath a marble tablet on the route
To purification. How he lingered there,
    Seeing his future.

He knew the punishment that he would suffer,
And suffer the more harshly for a vice
That strengthened him in flinty solitude and
    Humiliation.

However true it may be that his poem
Would never have been written had he not
Sealed off his soul from all discouragements,
    It's still a failing.

After all, time will show the difference
Between the soldier of true courage and
The one whose brazen recklessness would lead
    Men to their deaths.

The woman whom we think a connoisseur
Will soon enough be pegged as one that ooo's
At everything which sounds like foreign chocolate
    Or cellared wine.

Yes, there's a reason that Aquinas said
That all ambition is a sin. We can't,
While stiffened by that certitude it brings,
    See the cause clearly.

For, in the genius plotting intricate rhymes
To execrate the avarice and envy
Of those who burned his home and cast him out
    In wooded darkness,

Who passed a sentence on his children's heads,
And, in the gangly dancer without rhythm,
The politician with a taste for fame,
    It's all the same.

It's terrible that way, like power and beauty.
The mind can hover over its abyss,
Can hear the cataract roaring from below,
    And see its force

Shaping the rough stone of the world about us.
But there's no prior assurance; just the late
Judgment, once we're past change and stooped to read
    Our life's spread book.

Incense on the Air

I

The girls who came to campus for late Mass,
In skirts and woolen coats, would briskly pass
The gothic classroom buildings heaped with snow,
Shrinking into their scarves at each gust's blow.
The dome above glowed golden in the night
And bathed the church's steeple with its light.
Despite the hour and forbidding weather,
They'd chatter as they walked and laughed together;
And to evade what seriousness compels,
Would speak of liturgy as "smells and bells."
But then, they genuflect and cease such noise,
To chant and sing in unity of voice.
This lasts until the incense drifts away
And the pipe organ ceases in its play.

II

We understand the summoning of bells,
Whose soundings work upon us as might spells;
We know the power of note and harmony
Has something to it of divinity.
But what, in contrast, could the Church have meant
To make use of the homely stuff of scent?
I think back to a childhood party, where
I'd dressed in my best sweater, combed my hair,
Refused desserts and snacks lest, when I speak,
My teeth look stained or my fresh breath should reek.
But, as the evening trickled to its close,

I ate a single chip, and some girl's nose
Immediately sniffed the air; she quailed,
"What stinks?" For one taste my whole plan derailed.

III

Around this time, a friend at school smelled odd.
His mother'd fried filets of tainted cod;
A haze of oil and bad fish had made
Its way into his clothes and flesh and stayed,
Such that, though weeks had passed, I still could tell
He was in class behind me from the smell.
How fine the scent of pipe smoke on a suit,
And rank the remnant stench of rotted fruit.
Nothing reminds us we are animals,
That we are born of flesh and flesh appalls,
So much as smell, which stirs our deepest lust
Or, no less quickly, turns us in disgust;
It lures us just as light does to a fire
And counsels we are governed by desire.

IV

My parish priest once gave a homily
In which he claimed what stays in memory
The longest is a smell; it does not fade
But outlasts windowed scenes or words we've prayed.
It teaches eye and ear that, though they claim
Preeminence in what we learn and name,
The highest and the lowest things may find

More sensuous ways to enter in our mind,
And shape the soul by means we would disdain
As sharing less of reason than of pain.
Thus, incense on the air gives passing sense
An intimation of its permanence,
And leads us by instinctive power to rise
Like smoke into the gilded vault of skies.

O, Tamar

Has someone stopped you in the street to ask
A tourist's question? Have they begged you for
A dime, a drink from your secreted flask?

Have you stared on a tomb and marked time's score?
Or lost yourself in blurred casino light?
Pray to your god that he will salve that sore

Which slowly dries, then cracks again, the sight
Of which would drive the holy to depression.
How many begging hands have you, in spite

Or with a mirrored stare of self-possession,
Shoved aside, left to penury and the past?
You could not say, not even in confession.

Only that sore in memory will last,
Throbbing beneath the cover of your hand.
If someone knocked, you'd sit until she passed,

Then echo off the painted walls a bland
Excuse: you're ill and have no strength in store,
Or she had some quirk that you could not stand.

That silent girl, whose touch began to bore,
That crying one, who would not go away,
Until you set your jaw and shut the door;

That one with whom you wandered the whole day
Through the bright city when its streets were new,
And lent the heart a fullness none could say.

She parted finally and you withdrew
Within the seeping darkness that is you.

A Withered Tree

What form that we have found, in time,
    To give to time shape of what stands
Outside of time, as does a rhyme
    Outside a verse's measured bands,

Is all that we were looking for,
    As once we know it, we shall see
Its figure give out ever more
    The splendor that it is to be.

But, say we had just swept away
    All that was found by those before,
Just to allow a freer play
    To our desires, and nothing more.

Yes, say we had. Indeed, we did,
    And stand in arid poverty,
Our anguished gestures vain amid
    A furrowed field with withered tree.

The Fishing Camp

When the three men returned to the old camp,
After an absence of some thirty years,
They found much as they'd left it and remembered
The boats lined up and beached upon the sand,
A table perched above, its shape rough-hewn
And fish scales smeared into the weathered wood.
The clearing, ringed with pines and papered birches,
Was much the same, save that a new-built cabin
Stood near the shore, its posts of varnished cedar
Cut from the island's woods. A far cry, that,
From the cramped pile of gray and mortared logs,
Where he had toughed out nights in childhood.
    That afternoon, they sat out with their rods,
Sun flashing on the waves, and pulled the northerns
Out from the weedy shallows where they hid.
Freed from its tri-barbed lure, a walleye flopped
About the metaled belly of the boat.
But now, it was his hand that had to pin
It down and push the stringer through the jaws,
His hand that slit the sides, that night, and ran
A blade between the ribs and bright fillet.
    He sat for hours casting in the silence.
What came to him was sometimes very old.
One afternoon, out trolling near the shore,
Between the pines, he caught sight of the cabin
Where they had stayed on their first visits there,
A slope of bleached gray shingles lost in treetops.

At dusk, they ate what they had caught, played euchre,
Or stood out by the fire pit drinking rye,
Tossed fish heads smoldering among the logs.
    Up early, one day, while the others slept,
He dressed and grabbed a hacksaw off its nail,
Then hunted for a trailhead in the woods,
Remnant from years before, one he had followed,
When as a boy with uncle, father, brothers,
They'd dragged their weight up from the boats at dark
To sleep on plank bunks nailed to the back wall.
The loons would call and then recall each other
With their great moans across the shrouded water.
And other sounds, much nearer and more troubling,
Came to him, wakeful, limbs clenched still with fear,
As mice crept in through spaces in the logs
And ran along the creases of the cupboards,
Until they set a baited spring off snapping.
    He cut away the underbrush and found
The trail as it rose up the hill and through
The thick young woods, a trunk already fallen
Across it, dead limbs shagged with graying moss.
He came at last to where the door had been,
An empty mouth of shadow now, and entered.
The floor boards bowed beneath his step. He saw
The back wall haunted still by bunk frames, planks
Dusted with leaves, and cook stove scabbed with rust,
Its pipe detached and sagging toward the darkness.

And so, he stood in that familiar place
And knew he had arrived. But what it was
That he was looking for, he did not know,
And did not think that he could ever say,
But waited for it, there, within its walls.

The Darkness Coming

The world grows dim beneath
   A dark and lowering cloud,
Whose threat is that this vision,
   But no more, is allowed.

By whom, I ask? And wait.
   Who says the black must come?
Who crushes me beneath
   An arbitrary thumb?

All men are brought up short
   Before a door of stone;
The simple and the wise
   Agree we die alone.

But wisdom is a bird
   That rides on empty air,
As blind to what shall come
   As what dark wounds we bear.

It will not comfort you.
   So, do not comfort me,
As I stare through the dark
   Yet do not cease to be.

Teele Square Sunday Morning, Summer 2001

Just as I saunter down the front porch stair
    Into the brilliant flood of Sunday morning,
My collar pressed, pants creased, and without care,
    As if the world shrugged off all signs of mourning,
I catch sight of the dive bar on Teele Square.

And there, left blinking, helpless, lost in light,
    A man and woman who've just been kicked out,
Their cash all gone, shamed in each other's sight
    To exit, premature, some drinking bout
That now seems poised to finish with a fight.

The man calls out to me across the street
    To ask me for a dollar. I just smile
And pass on, but observe the morning heat
    Already overcoming hope and guile,
As their pink faces settle in defeat.

I can't be bothered, really, and arrive
    At Mass just as the bell begins to toll,
Squeezing into a back pew all alive
    With children fleeing their mothers' tired control.
One peers at me, then takes a sudden dive.

And here, an hour, we listen, sing, and pray.
　　The day is ripe and everything so clear,
We scarcely glimpse what else might come our way.
　　But when, months on, the dark headlines appear,
Joy stops, doors shut, and few of us will stay.

From *The Awful Disclosures of Maria Monk*

A novice never sees behind the gates.
It's only those who take the veil can go
Through doors and chambers closed off from the world.
The paintings in the room of the Three States
Reveal beasts gnawing on the damned below;
The saving flames where infant souls lie curled;
And, high above those glories where stars spin,
The priests and nuns alone enjoy God's light.
For, when nuns lie or steal, the deed turns white,
And priests, we're told, cannot commit a sin.

The nuns would say prayers, there, and wait in fear
For summons to the dark confessional.
Then, would they kneel before the seated priest
And loose their vices naked in his ear.
When silence fell, he'd hiss a subtle call
And take their buried flesh as his own feast.
My first night in the convent, Père Dufresne
Used me thus, keeping me until the dawn;
Two others did the same, as he looked on
To draw his pleasure from my speechless pain.

And there were other places, hidden deep
Beneath the chapel's ivory and gold.
Once, sent down to the cellar for some coals,
I tripped upon the trapdoor, where priests creep
In and out of the convent. I was told
Nuns who refused their wills were locked in holes
On either wall, arms bound and soft mouths stopped.
And in a darker place, I found the well,
Caked white with lime, where infant bodies swell—
Those born and baptized, strangled, and then dropped.

Sometimes, old country priests would come to preach,
Their faces flushed and mouths befouled with drink.
Others would show themselves in candlelight,
When evening prayers were done, and reach
Within our garments, while another'd slink
Into our beds and wait for us at night.
As one lay long upon me, I'd recall
The nuns who vanished, till I felt that bloom
Of some secreted life stirred in my womb
And thought how on its limbs white lime would fall.

Waking in Dresden

After Richard Peter's photograph of "Die Gute"

Her shoulders slumped beneath their heavy cloak,
Large hands outspread despite a shattered thumb,
The lady Goodness stares out on the smoke
And ruin below, and stands, as always, dumb.

More planes already drone on the horizon,
Their bellies pregnant with the bombs they hoard,
And as she rests her ever-restful eyes on
The ancient stones, they lose their long accord.

Everyone waking this peculiar morning
Must stare in wonder at what's been destroyed,
And put on stony black in silent mourning,
And, silent, ask what's left to be enjoyed.

The shame of the adulterer, the drunk,
The gambler who steals from his boss's till;
The shame in which the desperate are sunk
To give their flesh as toy to others' will;

The shame of him who said the cause was just
And let that payload whistle down to earth
And level all once risen back to dust,
Would seem to silence any talk of birth.

And here she stands, that sculpted Goodness, mute,
Incapable of speaking her own name,
As if all life were cut back to the root
And all that's left were to assign the blame.

But, in the silence of her weathered mind
And in some thousand other places, now,
Despite themselves, not to such wreckage blind,
The living wonder and start plotting how

They might rebuild what lies there and still burns.
They stare up from the shelter's opened door
And see the clearness of the sky returns
As dust of bone drifts round the brightening floor.

11

The lords of chivalry lay prone and shattered.
—John Crowe Ransom

What is our praise or pride
But to imagine excellence, and try to make it?
—Richard Wilbur

Saint Thomas and the Forbidden Birds

Beyond the window, morning sparrows made
Their song as if the whole world's goodness paid
Its plenty out for them and them alone.
The old saint heard their joy and squelched a moan
As his legs, stiff and heavy still with sleep,
Arranged themselves beneath his cassocked heap
Of belly. Where had he left off before?
He asked his three amanuenses, more
For their sakes—sprightly fingers, sluggish minds—
Than his. One said, with the forbidden kinds
Of birds and what their figures signified
For Moses, who charged the eagle's flight with pride.
    Aquinas sat a moment, mind withdrawn
From his mouth's taste of buttered loaves, the dawn
Without, the wish for more wood in the fire
To clear the frost from stone or to admire
The cool swift brilliance of all he said
As a swan plumes its white and well-turned head.
    He spoke: the long-beaked ibis feeds on snakes
To represent the man whom nothing slakes.
Feasting upon dead bodies' opened gore,
The vulture stands for all who thrive through war.
When Noah let the raven out to fly
It never did return, to signify
Such men whose souls are blackened by foul lust
Or who, unkind, won't pay back trust with trust.
The plodding puffball ostrich is that which
Figures all those weighed down with growing rich

And, hearing God's call, plant their soiled head.
Plovers like gossips on stray words are fed.
And who, on seeing the gull, does not admire
That its bright wings to heaven may aspire?
And yet, it wastes its hours adrift at sea
Gorging on fishy sensuality.
The hoopoe builds its nest on heaps of dung,
Just as despair's eyes view the world all wrong.
    He paused then, at the thought of earthly sorrows,
Our sickly past, incarnadine tomorrows,
The myriad things that whistle arcane truth
To please old minds and to instruct raw youth,
And bore down on his broken knees to pray
For such a world that had so much to say.

The Wisdom of Old Men

Up north, in winter, at the snowy deer camp,
The old men circled always near the fire,
Kept company with the crack of burning logs,
Their backs leaned in and smooth beneath plaid flannel.

And what they were about, I do not know,
Who darted in and out with skis or sled,
Or tramped knee-deep through silent, buried woods
To follow deer tracks miles from the cabin.

Their slowing bodies cool and stiff, they may,
With nothing left to do, have only sought
The heat that sweated from the barrel stove,
Its blackened sides, its flickering mouth ajar.

But, even in my youth, I saw them there,
As those charged with remembering days past,
With pondering the clockworks of the world,
As gear on gear ground through their ordered circles;

Those who descended to a place of freedom,
Where we may wonder at what has been made,
As Nestor, old, among the furious Greeks,
Sat by and spoke above his warming hands.

A Wedding Night

The blaring horns and drumbeat slipped away,
   As the great gilded door shut on the hall,
   But in my new wife's step and body all
Those fading rhythms lingered and held sway.
The hour late, the moon lit up our way
   Of worn-out cobblestone and granite wall,
   Of littered cup and dark graffiti scrawl,
All still and tranquil, far removed from day.

But, had we thought this hour a lasting peace,
   The city's vastness our joy's privacy,
A vagrant in a torn and soiled fleece—
Hunched in an alcove, rocking, one red eye
   Roving through darkness, till it fell on me—
Growled low and vacant, "You, you too, will die."

First Light

Why must I be the first one out,
  Each morning, houses sunk in fog
And locked along my lonely route?

The one whose unsuspecting face
  Will catch the threads that spiders draped
Across their darkened hunting place?

Who finds the oily-feathered crow
  With stiff claws upward, just before
It bloats with flies? I'll never know.

It's so conventional to prize
  Wakeful attention, we've grown blind
To how it wounds our naked eyes.

The Death of Cicero

A fluttering of wings and sudden pain
    Entered the guarded portals of his head,
Beneath its sheet, and woke him once again
    To find a ring of crows about his bed.
The sunlight shimmered on the distant sea.
      The birds cawed, restless, as though one divine
      Had sent their feathered darkness as a sign
That death approached and he must rise and flee.

His servants pulled him through the postern gate
    To ride in shadows to a waiting ship,
As if provision could slip free of fate.
    The litter jostled, sweat pearled on his lip,
And dust plumes, rising at the hastening feet,
      Settled upon his robe and graying beard.
      His valet's eyes were wild with what they feared
And found the blazing sails of Antony's fleet.

The carriage veered, then rattled to a halt.
    Its drape swung open to reveal two men;
They stood with swords drawn, ready for assault.
    He offered none, stretched forth his neck, and when
The blade was raised, told them, do what they would.
      His head dropped with his two hands, in the dust;
      Then, brought to Rome to answer Antony's lust,
All three were nailed, where Cicero once had stood.

But this, historians note, was not the end.
    Antony's wife would bow before that head
And, with her hairpin, pierce its tongue to send
    One final message to the noble dead:
Though they may speak with justice all their lives
    And bear death bravely, chatting of the soul,
    Power shall rule the world from pole to pole,
And nothing that defies its will survives.

Register

He took his place within the check-out line,
A loaf of bread, some milk, and batteries
Cradled against the paunch beneath his ribs.
His eyes fell vaguely on the sorted rows
Of chocolate, gum, and mints that lined the counter.
But, just behind, came some sharp click of tongue—
Briefer, but otherwise much like the sound
A plowman makes to coax his nag along
As it drags homeward through the roughened fields.
  It startled him from patient thoughtlessness,
The drift from wrinkly foil to bright orange wrapper
And glossy pill box, whose shapes occupied him
But which he viewed with no hint of desire.
He blinked and turned to see where it had come from.
  And there, not far away, just down the aisle,
Her head cocked back, distracted from its business
In searching through the cans of chicken broth,
A woman met his eyes. She met them, yes,
But without recognition, as if he
Were one among the stacks of labeled items,
Or, maybe, some great bulk that's strangely packaged,
Of doubtful provenance, but somehow sunk
Amidst the clutter of another's cart;
A lump one notices on accident,
And doesn't mean to, but, on instinct, thinks,
"That's not the sort of thing I'd buy for us."
  So much she seemed to say, while he stood suffering
Her gaze, a cold descending through his side,

Until, expressionless, she turned away
And spotted what it was that she had sought.
She lowered down, her fawn skirt smoothly slipping,
While one hand pressed the cloth against her thighs.
He watched her then. Her hand reached out. She drew
A can from somewhere lost within the shelves,
And turned its papered sides within her palm,
And ran a painted nail along the text—
With such a studied care, with such an interest—
To learn exactly what was held inside.

Elegy for a Tow Truck Driver

I'd watch you, neighbor, skulk behind the stands,
  Forever called away from your son's game
By wrecks, locked doors, a million small demands
  That faded when the speaker blared his name.
  But every fresh at bat would end the same.
    Then you would call him over, try to coach,
    Though all could hear the thinly veiled reproach.

We did not really understand the love
  Your son and daughter seemed to have for you,
But were relieved to see you take your glove
  And play a game of catch, or tie a shoe,
  Or other things that normal fathers do.
    They eased our conscience, when we heard you curse
    And judged, however bad, things could be worse.

So also, when we heard your wife had gone,
  We sympathized with her unhappiness.
And yet had thought that she might carry on,
  That, what we could not tolerate, she'd bless
  And soften your rough hide with her caress.
    But no. While you were curt and occupied,
    She'd found another who could warm her side.

One Sunday, in the springtime, after Mass,
    You staggered up to me, your face of frost
Speechless, as we stood in the greening grass.
     The months went on, and our paths seldom crossed.
     We heard by rumor what else you had lost,
       But nothing of the solitude and ache
       That brought the sleep from which you'll never wake.

O friend—if that's the word—I wish I knew
    That how you bristled through your years on earth,
Now that their mix of rage and cold is through,
    Was judged in someone's heart a thing of worth;
    That someone looked with fondness on your birth;
      That those you've left felt a judicious pain
      And would, if licensed, call you back again.

The Great State of Alaska

When we signed up to take a weeklong cruise,
Docking in scenic ports along the coast of
The Great State of Alaska, our friends cooed.
Their voice betrayed that kind of awe and envy
Which skips ahead a few weeks to the future,
Postpones and puts far out of mind the vision
Of hosts of angels in their fearsome brilliance
Descending, with their swords out, at the world's end.
It clears a place in thought to feel warm water
Lapping against one's slick, recumbent shoulders;
To sense a grip, both firm and gentle, as
The manicurist pares one's nails and smooths
Fingers grown stubbed and raw in winter air.
One's cheeks grow pink and young in such a thought.
    "You're going to *love* it," my friend Baxter said.
"Maybe you'll see a bear. *You'll* see a bear,"
He added, and then walked away, content,
Humming the same three notes in random sequence,
And vanished down the row of cubicles.
    My wife's great aunt, a veteran in such matters,
Advised that we could keep aboard the ship,
Even in port, to savor the buffets.
"That's when you get the best of it," she said.
"They have to carve as much beef as you want."
    From where we stood on deck, the world rose up
Above us with the sweep of granite bowls,
Trees at the base, which spread as thick as moss,
Then thinned until the weathered crown stood bare,

Pockmarked with remnants of the ancient snows.
The dome above us, gray and strained with clouds,
Hung like a marble tablet that had cracked.

    Old women, traveling without their husbands,
Smiled at us as if we were newlyweds.
During the banquet, as the ship left port,
One placed a hand of cool, soft, paper-thin
Flesh on my own and begged us, love each other,
As her third husband loved her, till the end.
My wife's eyes glistened, as if very moved.
I looked down at the woman's rings and nodded.

    We lived from meal to meal and each was long
And stuffing, the cuisine a far-flung hodgepodge
Of Thai, bread pudding, marinara sauce,
Great pork loins shaved beneath the orangey heat lamps,
And every seat, repose for those who'd come
For something so enduring it had sought
A stronghold here among the glacial bluffs.
Man's every urge, no matter how unlikely,
Including even the impossible
Desire to be thought wise regarding love,
Must somehow find its final refuge there.

    One morning, with the ship drawn into shore,
And mist still hovering where the mountains' backs
Like great indifferent beasts passed one another,
We trailed our fellow tourists down the dock
And headed inland toward the Mendenhall,
With various promised stops along the way.

The promises of one remain with me.
   The bus was crowded, quiet, save for coughs
That shook some septuagenarian
Out of his upright snooze. The gravelly roads
Lulled everyone toward sleep and my wife's head
Grew heavy on my shoulder, as we snaked
Around the bases of the coastal range,
Then up. The tired engine groaned and groaned,
Then stopped beneath a sky of towering firs.
   The driver sat there, as if lost, until
A man named Caleb bounded up the steps
And stirred us with his scratchy, shouting voice
To come, to follow him, at last descend,
Into a clearing. Back behind him lay
A massive greenhouse; all about us, posted
In earth like pillars, stood inverted trunks
Of spruce and hemlock, fluted bowls pitched upward,
And where, once, long ago, the roots had clutched,
Now overflowed the cheery, pied strands
Of wildflowers, blessed, dangling in the breeze.
   "It was no more than fifteen years ago,"
Caleb began, "A man the world now knows
As Ray came here and stood in this same plot.
The land about him was a waste and void.
The mountainside stood on the very brink,
One deluge more, of sliding out to sea,
Carrying with it what few broken stumps
And ruins from an old prospector's camp

50

Lay moldering about the steep terrain.
Mounting his excavator, Ray began to lodge
Into the dirt the trunks that had been felled.
He jammed their tops to earthward, plunged them deep,
And then, a lumberjack, he scaled those trunks,
And tossed into the elevated bowls
The seeds of every flower native here,
Till from such wreckage he had built this temple,
This place of florid beauty where we stand."
Caleb stood silent, overwhelmed with awe,
And watched the odd-ways grandeur sinking in.
        He was not done, but led us, rather, up
The ribbon of a trail through woods infested
With devil's club, with trees that rose up from
The soft, moss-coated, rotting humps of trunks,
Whose opened bark spilled out their nourishing guts.
It was a brilliant darkness, lush with life
Fed off of life, the slow stir of the air
Carrying the drift of salt in from the sea,
And punctuated by the scents of *rosa*
Rugosa and delphiniums that grew
Wherever sunlight reached the sloping floor.
        "Ray saved my life," our guide continued, "was
A second chance when I'd been lost and wandering.
He said, 'Your heart's broke, but you've got strong hands.'"
Tammy, Ray's wife, had done the same for others,
Apparently, and everyone who worked
The gardens owed their happiness to them.

Two orphan Eskimos had found a home
At last. An aged stevedore now spent
His days in charge of shaping up the bonsai.
A troop of girls who lost their way up north
By mystery and tragedy had come
To dwell as dryads over leaf and bud.
Beneath us, we heard someone chopping wood,
A strange hymn floating round each hack, as if
The rhythm of the earth had found its voice,
And mended every wound with harmony.
   At last, we came out on the mountain crest,
A broad pole shelter running near the cliff's edge,
And in the center of a gravel plain,
The black and smoldering remnants of a fire.
Again, he spoke. "Last night, beneath the stars,
The daughter Ray and Tammy gave the world
Was married here, and Ray performed the nuptials.
The drums, guitar, and dancing went till dawn.
I haven't slept myself, but most our staff
Is home this morning, or snuck off to nap
In one of those small hiker's lodges Ray
Constructed from the timber of old Juneau."
   The gravel bore the prints of faded feet,
I thought, and heard, or thought I heard, the sound
Of empty bottles juggled through the air
And laughter at some clownish jubilation,
As, in the spell of celebration, each
Whirled crowns of flowers in the vacancies.

I stared, from high, down on the continent
That opened wide before us, and could see
The foot trails leading pilgrims from afar,
From all the settled tracks and spoiled cities,
To here, where Ray and Tammy promised hope.
    Aboard ship once again, the dining room
Was lit aglow with golden candelabras;
A string quartet swayed slowly back and forth
And threaded all the air with some baroque
Melody leading somewhere that escaped me.
Women with elegance turned here and there,
Making their way between the feasting tables,
In gowns of blue or black, their breasts encrusted
With diamonds multiplying light on light.
Waiters flowed from the kitchen like champagne,
Their trays weighed down by plates of duck or lobster.
And just beyond the fullness of our chatter,
We saw the crowded heads of children laughing,
As with his dapper hat and gloves and cane
A coy magician summoned doves from nowhere.
    But even then, our exultation ripe,
Amid the clank of silver knives, the music,
Our heads grown light and vaporous and aswim
With cold and potent daiquiris, I heard
The coughs begin. And, in the days ahead,
The ship begun to roll as it pushed out
Far into the Pacific, all land vanished,
We lay upon the twin beds in our stateroom,

A deep and bellowing whoop within our chests,
Our bodies, churning, pulled away from us,
As if a drain had opened deep inside them,
As if they'd lose themselves within the deep.
    And, as I gripped the corner of my mattress,
I thought that, yes, the world may be a temple
That opens onto somewhere not itself,
Much as black water opens wide its doors
To take within itself the giant orcas
That leap, then twist and fall with straining backs.
    But no grove in its belly was a saved land,
No peak forever shelters us from nausea,
No place so fortifies itself that all
Becomes an everlasting dance of moonlight.
The engines sluicing water far below us,
And drawing us indifferently along
From port to port and none the final one,
I slowly came to know, there was, in fact,
No Ray, no Tammy, nor had ever been.

In the Fullness of Rhyme

Some say that it's okay to slant,
While other poets swear one can't.
The former conjure some excuse
For every assonant abuse,
The latter, rather, want good order:
A well-kept path and guarded border.
While one can't write by guide or chart,
The artist gives the law to art.

Thus, he must know enough of rhyme
To tell the caviar from the slime,
The well-coiffed head from the rough mullet,
The silver from the leaden bullet.
And though the bad he would not shoot,
What's good he'll pluck for his own fruit,
And every line will weigh with those
Sweet rhymes that our first poets chose.

The Prow of the House

The parlor lies beneath its settled dust.
The grand oak table in the dining room,
Long stripped of plate, cuillere, and candelabra,

Reflects the twilight like a polished tombstone.
And now, he stirs from stillness to ascend
Beyond the creak of stairs into the attic.

And though he knows there is no place to climb,
No stair to free him from the angered absence
Below, he breathes, and climbs it nonetheless.

The night is hot. A fan chirrs in the window.
The little tassel on the light goes *plink*
And casts a swinging shadow from the bulb.

Beyond, the paintings he's collected make
A crooked brickwork, leaning from their wires
With stripped-down frames, those pinks and greens
        and yellows.

One big hand sets the phonograph's fine needle
Into the groove and flips the broken switch,
Until some secret part at last turns on.

This is the secret part, the place of breathing,
Where all the empty beauties are enjoyed,
Where all the obtuse dead have reached and failed.

O, friend of such enameled solitude,
Who knows the joy of sound and colored glass,
Listen! His breath grows slower with the music.

Remember

We laugh to hear some crank philosopher
Once taught that learning is remembering,
   And what the soul knows now it knew before,
But buried with its birth, as if life were
A gradual return to everything
   Precious and splendid that our minds adore.

Yes, we know better—don't we?—that the curse
Of time runs like a cataract downhill:
   A surge of force that batters all to nothing.
The bad is carried blindly to the worse;
The dancer's lively bones will soon lie still;
   The spring itself at last will cease its frothing.

But then, I recollect my mother's face;
She, born among the railyards and skyscrapers,
   But having left them all long since behind,
Grew luminous, when someone from that place
Gave her a bundled stack of old newspapers
   And brought the absent city back to mind.

Or, picture, in some noisy Harlem street,
The eyes of Claude McKay spy ginger-root
   And tangerines piled on a grocer's cart;
At once, his heart flies from the city's beat,
Borne back to native boughs weighed down with fruit
   And prayers abandoned in pursuit of art.

He would, years on, seeking the paradise
The Russian Revolution brought to being,
   Find himself drawn, instead, within a church
And bowed before the altar's sacrifice:
That body of the dead man he'd been fleeing,
   As if it were the object of his search.

And so it probably was. For, what we seek
We cannot really know, or it would be
   Already ours; we trust in our desire
Not just to bear us through another week,
But as eyes wait for light's return to see
   And cold hands open on remembered fire.

In the Holding Cell

They took his belt and shoes, and led him in,
    The barred door rumbling back then slamming shut;
    Its clap, so brief and final, shook his gut
And echoed off the bunks of bolted tin.
Through sickly bands of gilded light he'd been
    Lifted by pinioned arms in silence, but
    He felt his head come round as steel cuffs cut
Lines roseate and stinging in the skin.

His brain still clouded, he could not be sure
What he had done or swallowed hours before,
    But jaw and shoulder ached, and swollen eyes read
All that was written on him through this lapse,
To piece the night together and, perhaps,
    Remember if the other guy were dead.

The Weakness of Men

The story is that men are getting softer.
They break down sobbing, hide a face beneath
A towel, after they've been benched, as if
A private room of terry cloth could shut
Out our contempt. They say that some men are
Afraid to lift a phone, to call the drug store
And ask the hours of the pharmacy.
They'll sit there, sunk upon the couch, and wait
For someone else to do it out of pity.

As Shakespeare must have known, or his Iago
Would never have pursued his jealousies
With such an anxious indirection, nor
His Edmund boast such god-defying strength
Only to try some good at his last whimper,
The feeble and ambitious are the same.
That one man seem most furious for glory
And stand above the bloodied corpse he's vanquished,
Is no sign he won't cower in a dress.

I think back half a lifetime, when I sat
At work, each day, in a small cubicle,
Waiting for some superior to ask
If I would type a contract, make some copies,
Or maybe nudge the office fern near sunlight.
Between us, we knew what I had been asked
Was servile, unimportant, even shameful,

Such that my betters would avert their eyes
And hasten back behind an oaken door.

It didn't help that some thought I was smart,
And asked for summaries of the books I read
At lunch, while eating in the conference room.
One man, who was a serious Jew, would quiz
Me on my knowledge of his people's faith,
So glad for the excuse to talk of it,
And yet, suspicious too I'd cribbed my answers
Or feigned my interest just to get ahead.
But, silently, we both knew that was futile.

One day, he mentioned he had written poems,
Their subject being the mysteries of God
Disclosed to those who'd braved their circumcisions.
He longed that they at last be read by someone.
He even brought them, locked in his worn briefcase,
And stood before me, wetting waxen lips,
Clutching the precious weight against his thigh.
But that was it. Once we faced one another,
Fear I'd dislike or steal them pulled him back.

His face came back to me, a few years later,
When, intern for a little magazine,
It was my job to open the submissions
And stack the cover letters with their poems
Or stories, for the editors to read.

And, letter after letter, said the same:
These are great poems. I know that you will love them.
It's so important they be published soon,
So, please, write back and tell me they've arrived.

Insistence bolstered by uncertainty,
The authors seemed as equally convinced
Of their great genius as their impotence
To make us see it. A great world's new birth
Lay waiting in their verse, they seemed to say,
Though, just beneath the paper's zealous flutter,
They'd sigh, "One more rejection and I quit."
There is a reason that the natural law
Says none may serve as judge in his own cause.

All men are made of glass. They pass through life
Knowing an hour comes when they'll be shattered.
But, yes, there was a time when guile or cunning
Could better hide from others what we now
Conceal by both self-flattery and silence
From just ourselves. Old tales of tragic courage
Founded in weakness gradually give way
To news reports of young men paled to ghosts
Who live in haunted terror of lost pride.

The Kitchen Stove

The autumn gusts have banked great claws of leaves,
   Of oak and maple, deep against the fence,
And torn a rusted gutter from the eaves.

The hour comes when faces, in dismay,
   Will pull the curtains, lock the door, and draw
Close to the slowly heating stove to stay,

Their backs curved like the chambered nautilus,
   Their thoughts within as wound and intricate,
And doubtful toward a world proved treasonous.

The ear rings in the silence of the room;
   The running gas keeps whistling its blue flame;
The heat swells outward from its iron womb,

And, in the fastness of this last preserve,
   One starts to think that every hope miscarries
And life's the off chance of an atom's swerve.

But thought, like heat, will build up and expand,
   Explodes at times, but also sometimes blossoms,
And makes our bodies answer its command.

That's why, alone, of all the things that are,
   Thought stands within and yet defies all fate,
And lights amid such darkness each new star.

It alone sees the planets as they move
   Are driven not by blind and brutal force
But drawn to order by eternal love.

Fire Light

The holy settlement of hours,
    Whose silence now descends like sleep,
    Who gathers us within its keep,
    And lets alone the hearth flames leap,
Affirms, for now, the only powers
Will be those we have claimed as ours.

A stillness, here, although the world
    Spins with the grind of stone on stone,
    Continues stripping flesh from bone,
    And tramples over prayer and moan,
While even those who now lie furled
Feel how its serpent's tail has curled.

So, flame, burn brighter for my eye
    Not in defiance, show, and pride
    Or to blot out all we've decried,
    But that our gaze might see inside
Some flicker of what's not yet nigh,
Where all is light and none shall die.

Sloth

*The notion of acedia means that a man does not, in the
last resort, give the consent of his will to his own being;
that beneath the dynamic activity of his existence, he is
still not at one with himself.*

—Josef Pieper

When autumn came, my grandfather set up
Behind a metal desk in his garage,
With slender ball-peen hammer and curved pick
   To hull and crack

The acrid mound of dusty, bruised, green husks
That each held in its core a small black walnut.
He'd gather them each year, while raking leaves,
   And bring them here.

Other men I have known had other passions,
To sell insurance or run clothing stores,
To coach a squad of boys to pitch and hit
   In summer league.

And we are so impressed by excellence,
By concentration, how it shuts the world out
And brushes off distraction with a rudeness
   Quite accidental,

That some have thought that this was our vocation,
The answer to the question why we're here,
And whose unceasing cultivation is
    Our happiness.

But even as a boy, when I would see,
Stowed in my idle laziness, the girls
Solicitous of every teacher's praise,
    Those busy bodies

Who volunteered to cook hot meals for old folks,
To tutor after school, or paint bright signs
For spirit week, I'd sense their flitting ache
    Of restlessness.

And though I felt rebuked by their goodwill,
And knew my brooding silence in the lunchroom
Was also discontent, if not distraction,
    And marked for shame,

I nonetheless thought they had fled the question
Posed by their selves, or pushed it off beyond
Tomorrow with assurance that they had
    Done what was asked.

And later, when I saw what Pascal wrote
About the king possessed of everything
Who would not have himself be left to sit
   In solitude,

For fear his roving mind's eye might return
Upon the glowering emptiness within
And there, cut off from glittering abundance,
   Find gnawing misery,

I knew that man, contemptible and great,
Could build a far-flung empery from worry,
An earnest moral sentence from a lie
   He tells himself;

And knew reflective anguish, in being thought,
Resembled more than humming outward deeds
What deed and thought both parody: that peace
   We fear to seek.

For it is silly, Aristotle says,
To think the gods live their eternity
Fiddling about with war or sex or money.
   They are all stillness.

No less must we, who crack our meat from shells
And earn commissions sweating at the office,
Set by our deeds at last for that pure act
  Of godlike rest.

III

A serious house on serious earth it is,
In whose blent air all our compulsions meet,
Are recognized, and robed as destinies.
And that much never can be obsolete . . .
                            —Philip Larkin

James' Book

One night, my oldest son comes on a quest
To ask if *he* can write a book. "Of course,"
I say, "What kind of story should it be?"
He does not know, but soon, as from some source
Flowing within the soil's depths, we see
A boy at the front door, a shadowy guest.

A trembling hand extends a folded note,
Which late that night, the boy will read in fear.
Days pass. He loads a pack with what he needs,
Till, in the dark, his footsteps frighten deer
Away and bring him to a place of weeds
And stones in the old forest. This we wrote.

And we wrote next his searching through the waste,
The flashlight burning blue on logs and moss,
As he brushed back thick leaves to look beneath.
Then his caked fingers felt the iron cross,
Jagged with rust and chill. He clenched his teeth
And dug the clay in which it was encased.

At last, then, in the insect-thrumming dark,
He gripped it firm and twisted while he pressed,
Just as the note instructs. An ancient gear
Somewhere below, disturbed from its long rest,
Begins to shift, the cross springs up, and here
Opens the door its buried heft would mark.

"What now?" I ask. He waits for me, unsure.
Dust rises on cold air from down below,
But his light cannot reach what lingers there.
He must descend beneath its circled glow
On a rough braided rope to find out where
The passage leads and what it holds in store.

That's all we've got. I tell him we'll need art
To fill out all the pages of our book.
"I'll do it. I can draw the cross," he says,
And you can see from his warm, wavering look
That just to make that shape in crayon is
All he dares try—but he can't wait to start.

For Russell Kirk

The panting ideologues who pace their rooms
    Hear the word "order" and cry out in fear
That it is just a shibboleth for dooms
    As yet unseen but whose goosesteps they hear.
But, it is better taken as the word
    A bachelor mulls as he writes through the night
And which enables him, some thought occurred,
    To set it down in prose both broad and tight.

While others lapse upon their couch in dreams,
    Or type with bloodshot eyes and whiskey breath,
The ordered man appears as his work seems
    Fixed with a permanence to outlast death.
    Cathedral glass has color and firm border,
    As do such men conformed by love to order.

First Words

And then I resolved that thenceforward I would choose
for the theme of my writing only the praise of this most
gracious being. But when I had thought exceedingly,
it seemed to me that I had taken to myself a theme which
was much too lofty, so that I dared not begin.

—Dante

A pounding in his heart gave him a shove—
   More like a slap—and set his mind to writing,
Ladies who have intelligence of love.

He had not slept for nights, but stared above
   Him at the ceiling till, upon its lighting,
A pounding in his heart gave him a shove,

As one might a small skiff mired in a cove
   To dare the open sea however blighting.
Ladies who have intelligence of love,

Such words ensnare his mind but his hand move,
   Scoring in strokes the page with his inditing.
A pounding in his heart gave him a shove;

Yes, soon, he'd claim an angel or a dove
    Had whispered such words to him without flyting—
Ladies who have intelligence of love—

But we who've felt love's pain know what sort of
    Rough wrangling he'd been suffering and fighting.
A pounding in his heart gave him a shove:
Ladies who have intelligence of love.

After a Line by Maurice Scève

So far the one I love surpasses me
That, even writing this, I stop and wince,
   And, having finished once, I start again,
And yet again, and have done nothing since,
   But scratch out faulty phrases with my pen,
So far the one I love surpasses me.

So far the one I love surpasses me
That every metaphor dissolves to dust
   And disappears upon the vacant air,
Rather than stretch out as a bridge I trust
   To bring across the one who draws my stare,
So far the one I love surpasses me.

So far the one I love surpasses me
That all the rattling refuse in my sack,
   The stray flames flickering about my brain,
Which I had saved for this, come hurtling back
   Reflecting not her mind but my heart's pain,
So far the one I love surpasses me.

So far the one I love surpasses me,
My listeners think it all sad fantasy
   Conceived by one who lives too much alone,
And forms of shadows what can no more be
   Than could a crown of stars or wisdom's throne,
So far the one I love surpasses me.

Australia

Sluggish with Pennsylvania summer rain
Slapping and splattering against the drive,
I sit, incapable of anything.
My daughter asked me, weeks ago, to write
A poem about Australia, and I
Agreed, but not with that clean kind of yes
That means itself, but with some other kind,
More like a groan of dread, my chest collapsing.
    What did she mean by that—Australia?
A drawing up of heavy chains from depths
Where they lay oxidizing and forgotten,
Whatever once was linked at their end vanished?
    She's heard the stories of my boyhood there;
The getting out of punishment, the cane
The headmaster would brandish left to idle,
Stood in a corner of his office, only
Because by cunning and selective silence
I dodged the visit that had been commanded.
The time I fed a neighbor boy wet sand,
Calling it chocolate. As the sound of grit
Between his teeth came from that just-closed mouth,
I asked him if he wanted any more,
And he said, yes—just that same kind of yes
I gave, as if the word "Australia"
Were sand now settling just behind my tongue
And slowly growing round and rich with nacre.
    Or was it not myself, but rather other
Things in their upside-down, pineapple strangeness?

The coming in from play outdoors to find
The lizard whose tail I had just whisked off
The week before, while sweeping the garage,
Caught frozen on the stairwell wall, its eyes
Locked on me, waiting for my hand to move,
Before it darted toward the green shag carpet
And disappeared. That other time, when hidden
In the back garden, absolutely hushed,
Concealed within a thorny, violet bush,
Knowing that, there, my brothers could not find me,
I looked down where my hand had gripped a branch,
And found amid a thickened weave of web
The rounded, gashed hump of a redback spider.
    A place where weird concocted creatures lived—
The kangaroos and platypuses, emus—
And not just lived, but wandered, defecating.
The platypus discharging as it swam
Those slender remnants of whatever they eat
Along aquarium glass, then turned its back
And sank from sight within the dank green water.
The giant bird who ambled up to me,
Until I threw my seed down out of fear,
And watched it sweep its long neck down to feast,
While splattering its three-horned feet with waste.
    I don't know if she wants what I brought back
On purpose, wool clipped off a sheep at school,
The boomerang our next-door neighbor gave me,
Or what I could not mean to see, but saw:

What forced itself upon me with its oddness,
As if to show that nature's jerry-rigged,
Holding its giant bird head high with pride
To be so awkward and yet possible,
So plainly misassembled and yet ambling,
Defying expectations like the joey
That crawls its mother's pelt to find her pouch.

Elizabeth to Her Cousin

After Jacob of Serug

Blessed are you, O Maiden; blest
    The fruit which dwells within your womb,
Beloved in that holy rest
    Whose secret comes to sacred bloom.
And blessed is this virgin birth
    Which shall uproot sin from the earth.

Who grants this favor to me now,
    That you should come, O Blessed One,
Bearing the great who is made low?
    By his own will this thing is done.
The mother of a king, and yet,
    It's at my wooden door we've met.

Let every mouth speak out your praise,
    And all the seraphim stand shaken.
Your womb contains the brilliant rays
    That from a living flame shall waken
This world, whose sleep in sin-black night
    Gives way before new life and light.

The gardener who clears the thorns;
    A lion's cub whose jaws shall roar
Louder than all of Joshua's horns,
    And drive all craven wolves before:
Such is the sun that all shall see
    Arise from you as from the sea.

But who am I that you should come
  Bearing the one who made the world,
Who is its savior and its sum,
  And yet within you now lies curled?
I am unfit, Ancient of Days,
  To welcome you or speak your praise.

But, Lady blest and full of grace,
  I see your beauty and rejoice;
The radiant flush upon your face,
  A living water in your voice,
Disclosing what alone you know,
  That light and word within you grow.

No angel spoke this truth to me,
  But he who dwells within me stirred
The moment that my eyes could see
  Your distant form, and my ears heard
Your call, as down the hill you came,
  Bearing that secret, ancient flame.

Sunlight

On asking the philosophers,
  What is the sun?, we get in answer,
"An angel perched"; "a heap of furze

Some god has set ablaze"; "a burning
  Iron that melts from sword to plow
To spearhead with the seasons' turning."

And some wise soul guffaws at them
  Or, condescending, calls it "poetry"
To disbelieve but not condemn.

Thus does the minute judge the hour,
  Dismissing that primordial truth
That only speaks with figural power.

An Encounter

I've been away all day, and coming home—
I can't believe it—all the kids are leaping
To tell me what's transpired in my absence.
They're at the store together, five of them
Propped in the shopping cart or following it,
Their mother slowly leading down the aisle,
To get the toilet paper, bread, a roast,
And, for the birthday coming on the weekend,
A heaping cake, balloons, and paper plates.
She moves in silence, all her thought consumed
By what is on her scratched-down list and what
Has been left off—so frazzled, hurried out
The door, and trying to get things loaded up
And back before I come in from the train.
    But then they hear a noise, and all the kids,
And then my wife, look round and see a woman
Who stares at them, then whispers to her son,
A smile of contempt upon her lips,
Then laughs and whispers to the boy again.
    Rehearsing this, the family's like a flame,
Burning to share their righteous indignation.
But, listening and trying to imagine,
I just grow restless, wishing I had been there,
Had put myself before that gaze of scorn,
That woman—who was *she*?—and her rank spawn,
To step between them, shame those eyes and mouths.
But it was just a passing episode.
The kids take turns retelling, while my wife

Insists that it was hardly anything.
    Meanwhile, in days to come, I place myself
Again into that scene—again, again.
I write myself into it, stage it over.
I play the whole thing over with me there,
And no one else, to meet those viewless eyes
And turn them back upon their lousy selves.
Rage grows, achieves its pitch, then wears away,
And all within a void of fantasy
From which I scarcely feel myself emerge.
    And when I come at last back to myself,
I find the children shouldering each other,
Their elbows jockeying to reach the front,
To get their fingers on that opened sack,
Which in the clamor now begins to spill
Upon the kitchen counter, then the floor,
In blue, in red, in yellow, pink, and green,
The tight and shriveled petals of balloons.
The children clutch and squawk with such a racket,
Pouncing upon the colors as they fall,
I cannot tell if it is joy or rage.

For Martha

Busy with many things, I know you are,
　　And watch you turn away and close the door.
I see it in the way you drive your car,
　　In how things clutter on your kitchen floor.
Someone will advertise new ways to mend it,
　　To find a method and a discipline,
But you and they both know you'll never end it,
　　Just fall for schemes to get rich or grow thin.

Even so, beneath the stirrings of your heart,
　　There lies some memory of peace and stillness,
An image uncontrived by human art
　　That makes this life seem one persistent illness.
　　Turn inward then, just as those teachers say
　　Who make of silence words by which to pray.

Seeds

We all have heard the parable of the sower:
The man who goes out with his bag of seed
And scatters it on path and stone and soil.
How rare, we think, for work to come to fruit,
The world about us hard and parched and stingy.

We look at Malthus, upright in his pulpit,
The flint of withered cheek and weathered brow,
And almost wonder why it took so long
For men to figure out the inner truth
Of things is parsimony and decay.

The seeds themselves object to this, of course,
The lilac seed that grew amid my maple,
Its gaudy purple blossoms bent beneath
A canopy of broad-tipped, spreading leaves,
The two together tangled in their living.

As if in generous revenge, a maple
Sapling has sprouted in our pink azalea,
And wind has found out every hillside furrow
To pack with dandelions, who raise bright heads
On stout necks in defiance of all doubt.

They rustle with the cool air of the spring
And give themselves away with silver plosions.
But so does everything. The children racing
Around the playing field's new-painted diamond;
The hand moved by some vision to draw angels;

The song escaped a passing car's cracked window
That catches in a woman's ear and, though
She's late for her appointment, starts her humming;
A couple resting on a bench, their child
Asleep, the stroller rocking back and forth.

All things declare their being and their goodness
By going out beyond themselves like seeds,
Their almost endless circle of new birth
Much like the turn of planets and of stars
That imitate the circle of their source.

By That Heart Known

A Hymn for Saint Philip Neri

The young man in his cell
   Receives his guest
Who all his heart should tell
   And leave there blest.
In quiet company
We shall a marvel see
As every thought shall be
   By that heart known.

To Rome the pilgrims came
   Poor as God chose them.
He calls to each by name;
   He serves and knows them.
Then with his friends he'll stray
Along the Appian way
In lively talk and play,
   His sweet grace sown.

With all who roamed the street
   The saint would tarry,
Each sorrow he should meet
   Was soon turned merry.
Yet he prayed with the dead
In their stone-chambered bed,
Till flames his great heart fed
   And its life grown.

Who is this fool? they jeer;
   He won't reply,
For that's how he'd appear
   So to deny
All claims to holiness,
Which are vain weights that press
On one who'd simply bless
   Poor hearts alone.

For him it was such ease
   To turn to God,
His joyful jests would cease
   And his head nod,
As he passed far beyond
This world of which we're fond,
And freed from every bond
   His heart was flown.

Who stirs the old man's room
   Finds him in prayer,
But with his laughter's bloom
   Leaves pain and care.
Into his company
The great and wretched flee,
As, in this oratory,
   We are his own.

At Season's End

For Cecilia Rae

Take down the ornaments and let them drop
    Atop each other in the crate,
Amid loose rifts of glitter and bent hooks
    Where, for another year, they'll wait.

And, turn the tree, unwinding the dimmed lights,
    Then wrap them in a tighter spool,
Before the heap of branches is dragged out
    To bridge the gutter's icy pool.

The soft matte warmth of bold poinsettia blooms
    Dries in one corner to sick green,
And even Ceci, lost in her dolls' world,
    Knows what her father's motions mean.

The room grows bare, the floor is swept of needles,
    But her new dollhouse full of voices
Raised up in imitation of those carols
    We sang last week. Each doll rejoices.

Yes, every moment is piled up and stored
    In attic, basement, or in mind,
As if time, fled upon its fading note,
    Left something of itself behind.

High Seriousness

Having emerged, at last, from the hot train,
Its silence broken only by newspapers
And the conductor, shifting down the aisle
   To pluck each fare

Pinched on its perch atop the canvas seats,
We come out where the evening brightness cleanses,
The row of maples by the station woven
   With cool, clear air.

And even now, across the road, old couples
Follow the hostess to an early seating
On the trattoria's stone patio
   With white-draped tables.

If you should pass, you'll see a waitress lift
The pinot grigio from its tub of ice
And pour a slender splashing liquid light
   To fill the glasses,

But I, with sweating collar, close-cinched tie,
Recall, two decades back, the cloudy slates,
Stiff chairs, and clanging radiators of
   The cloistral classroom:

Those arguments we had about the art
Of poetry—its craft, what lasts, what fades—
And my mute glare of anger toward those who
    Sat there indifferent.

How could they not see our lives staked on rhyme,
A civilization's rise in Sidney's meter?
Not see the law of being mirrored in
    Well-ordered words?

And passing, after, by the squat frat houses,
Still in a muffled rage at some obtuse
Remark or pedantry tossed off, and smarting
    My own words' failure,

I'd see the boys out idle in their yard
Bare-chested, football arcing back and forth
Between them, as if just there to remind me
    I had no time.

No time for that loose spread of fingers, no,
But only for the tight pinch and strict grip
Of pen and book, when darkness closed down hard
    On autumn study.

Among Americans, Tocqueville had noticed,
Every idea was softened by the chuff
Of humor, as if they drew back from faith
   Like Abram's knife;

He died convinced, through unbelief and anguish,
They'd lost thereby the last high seriousness,
Which faded, now, away, with the old order,
   Her sabers trampled.

Some decades on, that stern schoolmaster, Arnold,
Felt stung straight through the heart and blushed to read
Of Palemon lusting over a silly girl
   Spied in the garden;

Or of the Miller's man who came in darkness
To his beloved's sill and kissed her ass.
What kind of sober lesson could that give
   To all the vulgar?

The rioters who forced the gates of Hyde Park?
The liberals from the mills of Birmingham?
We need an image higher, more austere,
   To summon us.

We need, in fact, to be thrown down, horse bolting,
And blinded by the gravid flash of truth,
Which suffers no glib smiling, if we're ever
   To heed our calling.

We need to sense that our first intuition
Of truth is something worth descent through darkness,
Though it demand our solitary parting
   From all we've known.

But, when we rise, we come to a spread table,
Where laughter, light as music on the air,
Weaves through our argument. We sit at leisure,
   And lift our glasses

To one another, their rims radiant
And bringing a cool sweetness to our lips,
Till all we'd guarded with astringent strictness
   Returns as joy.

The Love of God

The love of God is earlier than man,
Present to us before we were to it.
The love of God sustains and nourishes
And puts in being what had never been
Save that it was first loved, and being loved

Had being at all. The love of God comes down,
And walks among his creatures as their friend,
And dies among his children in their rage.
The love of God has journeyed into hell
And all once closed is opened by that love.

The love of God stands fearsome over our heads.
The love of God has entered in our breasts;
And there, the love of God will dwell, where he
Was from the first the center of ourselves,
For all things turn about the love of God.

Snowfall

Descend and gust and fall,
In silence and in squall,
   Till every light's obscured
   And all the earth interred
By snow that covers all.

What depth of purity,
What answer to what plea
   Is brought by such a storm,
   In giving fairest form
To all the eye may see?

For, though the sudden cold
Seems fierce as it takes hold,
   We sense within it, grace
   To clarify the face
Of all that had grown old.

So, fall in flakes, descend
And to the dark earth lend
   An image from above
   Of that approaching love
Which comes to heal and mend.

Vanished Fire

Bright burning embers fall to somber coals,
    And, in the morning light, the emptied nook
    Seems the sole darkness on which eye may look,
In such a room, where whites make brilliant wholes
Of drapes and spreading carpet, couch and china bowls.
    But there, that lately-burning mouth
    Now speaks of shadow and of drouth,
As if to shame our dog-eared fireside book;
    Its story of a marriage made
    And sentiments that never fade,
    Brought by the fire's fainting flash
To seem as fragile as a bough of ash.

And ash, indeed, the world has often been.
    The much-loved friend and confidant, in time,
    Returns but to remind you of some crime
Of youth, committed while the mind was green
But knew already what the errant will could mean;
    The boy you followed home to beat
    Then made a coward's quick retreat,
Your knuckles smeared with sweat and dust and grime.
    He represents what you'd forget,
    The foolish plot or night's regret,
    Not with his words, but in his face
Whose lines seem like a script the eye may trace.

No shortage of reminders such as this;
     They come, alas, just when some touch of pride
     Has made the world seem glass on which to glide;
Just when we think that there is no abyss
Waiting to greet our blithe face with a sloppy kiss.
     That thing you said to someone's harm
     Which you had thought a sign of charm,
But now see no one near you could abide;
     The casual dishonesty
     To show the world that you were free
     Now shows itself for what it was:
A mere enchantment at one's own applause.

These, we know, are the wounds of vanity.
     The voice within reports that we are great
     And lulls us to believe it with sweet bait
That feeds the hungry ear on fantasy,
And shouts down every voice that dares to disagree
     With what it offered as the case.
     But then, that voice will spin in place
And where it praised before, now snarls with hate
     At how the world's a mass of flies
     That procreates and feeds and dies,
     That savors vice, that lives for power
And never knows a kind or noble hour.

Yet, even in the silence of the mind,
    Chastened and clarified, we sense indeed
    The world's a wilderness where all things bleed,
Its cities bombed, its people scarred and blind,
Its fruits grown overripe and eaten to the rind
    Though all still hunger. Who could say
    It's just imagination's play
That finds a father's murder or his greed
    Endemic to the life we know?
    Whatever else the world may show,
    It finds time for the child whom
A cold indifference severs from the womb.

These ashes in the fire, these half-burnt logs
    Left blackened, riven, and disintegrating
    Behind the scorched and bent and weathered grating
Will give themselves away as analogues
For grave and petty wounds the psyche catalogues.
    If evil's the enduring fact
    So is this way our minds react
To find out figures for our contemplating,
    This doubling of things as signs
    Which opens them as it defines
    And helps the intellect to see
Even within the darkest mystery.

Such is the strangeness of most beauty's birth.
    Amid the battered armor on the field,
    Some victor paints a crest upon his shield
And vows to treat the weak as things of worth.
A fixed stare on the crumbling deep of blackest earth
    Will find concealed within that sight
    The thought of everlasting light.
The open wound shows how it may be healed.
    We would not choose to learn this way.
    Why can't the mind know only day?
    Surely the form of truth does not
Require acquaintance first with death and rot.

Imagine, for a moment, such a place
    As saints and wise men sometimes tell us of;
    A place not here, but, in a sense, above,
Where all is light and plenitude and grace;
No abstract thing, it meets us with a radiant face.
    On sight, we know that we are blest
    To find in it perpetual rest.
This alone is the object of our love,
    And could we know it from the start
    The soul would never once depart.
    But, here, in battered things, we find
Faint traces that will summon it to mind.

What, for some other sort of creature, may
 Seem a distraction from that elegance,
 For us has the necessity of dance,
Its suffering that reorders us for play,
Its discipline that strengthens those who first obey.
 Some of us sense it and draw back,
 Refuse to name this thing we lack,
But savor its sensation of a trance,
 As if that were the most of it,
 And not a sign to make us fit
For that long passage now begun
Which scatters us before it makes us one.

How curious that what transcends all things
 Should choose to hide itself within them too,
 And pierce the sky's finality of blue.
What seems the last is but the first of rings
That from the dark whirls outward on extended wings.
 Thus in the empty living room,
 Out of the vanished fire's tomb,
Such veering thoughts will sometimes come to you.
 They settle in the memory
 Whose eyes, with failing vision, see
 Inside those ashes that appear
A brilliance, distant, foreign, and yet clear.

IV

Farewell to Berwyn

Somewhere, a dog is barking in the night,
    But our house idles still.
Our plastic dumpsters rolled down to the curb,
    Some hours ago, they will
Stand stout in their perched state of burdened waiting.
    We have some hours to kill.

Our pile this week is bigger than the rest,
    Heaped with a rocking horse,
Some outgrown clothes, the spindles of a chair
    That came apart, of course,
Just as we started packing: fate, it seems,
    Compels us now by force.

Our first night in this house, I came outside
    With emptied boxes flat
And saw how much the clarity of stars
    Asked to be wondered at.
What luck, I thought, that we had settled in
    So graced a habitat.

The stars grow old far slower than we do.
    They'll still be shining down
After I latch this door a final time
    And idle with a frown,
Doubting that we have made the proper choice
    To leave our house and town.

But now, the hour, suspended, swirls with clouds,
    The sky reflecting grey;
The children's voices clamor in my head,
    To unsay all I say,
To call the movers and call off the truck
    And tell them that we'll stay.

What is it makes me disregard those words
    And my own aching doubt?
A stubborn heart that, where it ought to yield,
    Puts fantasies to rout—
And I, the one who locked the door at night
    To shut the darkness out?

About the Author

James Matthew Wilson is the Cullen Foundation Chair in English Literature and the founding director of the MFA program in creative writing at the University of Saint Thomas. The author of twelve previous books, his collection of poems *The Strangeness of the Good* (2020) won the Poetry Book of the Year award from Catholic Media Awards. The Dallas Institute of Humanities and Culture awarded him the Hiett Prize in 2017; Memoria College gave him the Parnassus Prize in 2022; and the Conference on Christianity and Literature twice gave him the Lionel Basney Award. He serves as poet-in-residence of the Benedict XVI Institute, editor of Colosseum Books, and poetry editor of *Modern Age* magazine. He lives with his wife and five children in Grand Rapids, Michigan.

Acknowledgments

Versions of these poems first appeared in the following journals and magazines.

First Things: "To an Unborn Child"; "Return to Saint Thomas"; "Waking in Dresden"; "Saint Thomas and the Forbidden Birds"; "Elizabeth to Her Cousin"; "For Martha"; "By That Heart Known"

Alabama Literary Review: "Self-Possession"; "The Wisdom of Old Men"; "Elegy for a Tow Truck Driver"; "The Fullness of Rhyme"; "At Season's End"; "High Seriousness"; "The Love of God"

Anglican Theological Review: "The Garden"

National Review: "M.A.C."; "Lilacs"; "First Light"; "A Wedding Night"; "For Russell Kirk"; "First Words"; "Snowfall"

Forma: "Twilight"; "The Fishing Camp"; "Australia"

Reformed Journal: "Cracks"; "The Prow of the House"

Hudson Review: "Ambition"

Doxology: "Incense on the Air"; "Fire Light"

Presence: "O, Tamar"

Agonist: "A Withered Tree"

Trinity House Review: "The Darkness Coming"; "After a Line by Maurice Scève"

North American Anglican Review: "Teele Square Sunday Morning, Summer 2001"; "Register"; "The Weakness of Men"; "Sunlight"; "An Encounter"

The Lamp: "From *The Awful Disclosures of Maria Monk*"
Notre Dame Review: "The Great State of Alaska"
Evangelization & Culture: "Remember"; "The Kitchen Stove";
    "Seeds"
Wine Cellar Press: "In the Holding Cell"
Literary Matters: "Sloth"
America: "The Death of Cicero"; "James' Book"
Plough: "Vanished Fire"
The New Criterion: "Farewell to Berwyn"

The author would like to thank A.M. Juster, Dana Gioia, Ryan Wilson, Daniel Jabe, and, as always, Hilary Wilson for their helpful editorial advice in the revision of these poems. Thanks also to Bill Thompson, Tod Worner, and Mark C. Henrie for their different kinds of support in the making of these poems.